The Big Red Apple

David Tunkin

Illustrated by Peter Paul Bajer

There once was a big apple tree,
with big red apples.
On the lowest branch hung the biggest,
reddest apple of them all.

The big red apple was not happy.
"I want to fall off the tree," he said.
"I want to go off and see the world."
But the big red apple did not fall off the tree.

One morning, a little girl saw the apple tree.
"I am going to pick the biggest and reddest apple,"
she said. "Then I am going to eat it."
"Oh no," said the big red apple.
He gave himself an extra hard shake.

Thump!

The big red apple fell to the ground.

"I am off to see the world at last," he said.

He gave himself another shake

and rolled down the hill.

The big red apple had not gone very far
when a big black crow saw him.
"I will eat that big red apple," said the crow.

"Oh no you will not," said the big red apple.
"I am off to see the world."

Just as the crow swooped down
to pick up the big red apple, the apple rolled
under some bushes and down the hill.

The big red apple had not gone very far
when an old brown horse saw him.
"I will eat that big red apple," said the horse.

"Oh no you will not," said the big red apple.
The apple rolled down the hill.

At the bottom of the hill there was a man.

He saw the big red apple rolling along.

"Look at this big red apple," he said.

The man put the big red apple in his basket.

"Oh no," cried the big red apple.

"Now I will never see the world."

The man got on his bike to ride home.

Bump!

The bike hit a big hole

and the big red apple bounced out of the basket.

The apple landed in a big hole.

The apple lay there for a long, long time.

Leaves and dirt filled the hole

and covered the big red apple.

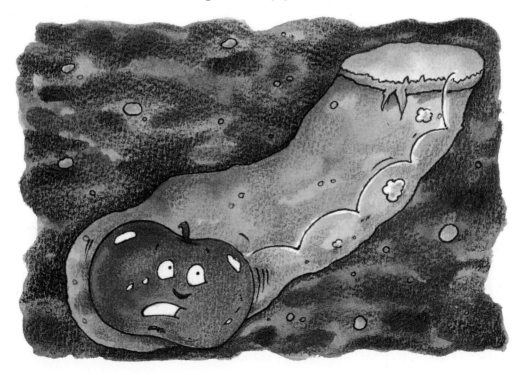

In the spring, a new tree began to grow in the field.
The tree had a little trunk and branches,
and green leaves.
The tree said, "I was once a big red apple,
but now I am a little green apple tree."

The apple tree grew taller and taller.

One day, a little girl climbed high up in the branches.

"I can see the whole world from up here," she said.

This made the apple tree very happy.